Plants are living things

Bobbie Kalman

Crabtree Publishing Company

www.crabtreebooks.com

Created by Bobbie Kalman

Dedicated by Crystal Sikkens
To my close friends Steve, Kari, Alanna, Cheyenne, and Aiden

**Author and
Editor-in-Chief**
Bobbie Kalman

Editors
Reagan Miller
Robin Johnson

Photo research
Crystal Sikkens

Design
Bobbie Kalman
Katherine Berti
Samantha Crabtree (cover)

Production coordinator
Katherine Berti

Illustrations
Barbara Bedell: pages 8 (all except fern), 17, 18, 24 (apples, shoots, and tubers)
Bonna Rouse: pages 6, 7, 8 (fern), 10, 16, 24 (bulb, cell, and flower at top)
Margaret Amy Salter: pages 20, 24 (flower in middle)

Photographs
© Dreamstime.com: pages 1 (girl), 22 (top)
© iStockphoto.com: front cover, pages 5 (right), 10, 11, 14, 15, 22 (bottom), 23 (left), 24 (middle left)
© ShutterStock.com: back cover, pages 1 (plants), 4, 5 (background and left), 7 (bottom), 8, 12, 13 (top right and bottom right), 16, 18, 19, 20, 21, 24 (middle right and bottom right)
Other images by Digital Stock, Photodisc, and TongRo Image Stock

Library and Archives Canada Cataloguing in Publication

Kalman, Bobbie, 1947-
    Plants are living things / Bobbie Kalman.

(Introducing living things)
Includes index.
ISBN 978-0-7787-3233-4 (bound).--ISBN 978-0-7787-3257-0 (pbk.)

    1. Plants--Juvenile literature. I. Title. II. Series.

QK49.K327 2007   j580   C2007-904246-5

The Library of Congress has cataloged the printed edition as follows:

Kalman, Bobbie.
    Plants are living things / Bobbie Kalman.
       p. cm. -- (Introducing living things)
    ISBN-13: 978-0-7787-3233-4 (rlb)
    ISBN-10: 0-7787-3233-9 (rlb)
    ISBN-13: 978-0-7787-3257-0 (pb)
    ISBN-10: 0-7787-3257-6 (pb)
    Includes an index.
    1. Plants--Juvenile literature. I. Title. II. Series.

QK49.K155 2008
580--dc22
                                        2007027226

Crabtree Publishing Company

www.crabtreebooks.com   1-800-387-7650

Printed in Canada/072013/TT20130703

Published in Canada
Crabtree Publishing
616 Welland Ave.
St. Catharines, Ontario
L2M 5V6

Published in the United States
Crabtree Publishing
PMB 59051
350 Fifth Avenue, 59th Floor
New York, New York 10118

Published in the United Kingdom
Crabtree Publishing
Maritime House
Basin Road North, Hove
BN41 1WR

Published in Australia
Crabtree Publishing
3 Charles Street
Coburg North
VIC, 3058

Contents

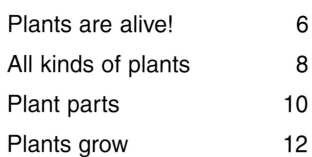

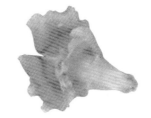

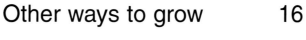

Living things need...

Living things need air. Living things need water and food. Living things need sunshine. Living things need places to live and grow. People are living things. Animals' are living things. Plants are living things, too. Plants need air, water, food, and sunshine.

Plants need places to grow. Some plants grow in soil. Some plants grow in water. Which of these plants is growing in soil? Which plants are growing in water?

hyacinth

water lilies

5

Plants are alive!

All living things are made of tiny parts called **cells**. Plants are made of cells, too.

plant cell

Cells are tiny. We cannot see them with only our eyes. We need a **microscope** to see them. This boy is using a microscope to look at plant cells. This is what he sees with the microscope.

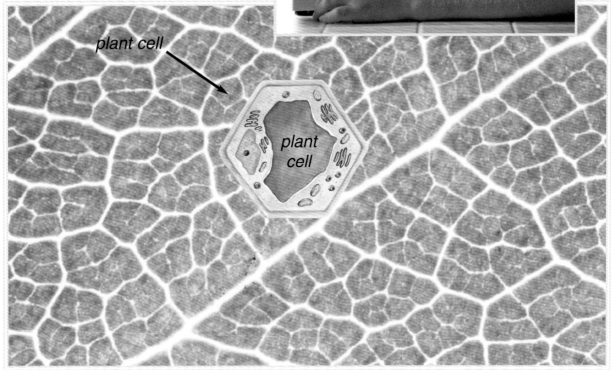

plant cell

plant cell

All kinds of plants

flower

Flowers are plants. Grasses are plants. Weeds are plants. Ferns are plants, too. Is this deer a plant? What kind of living thing is it?

grasses

weed

fern

Trees are the biggest plants. Some trees are as tall as skyscrapers!

Plant parts

Most plants have **roots**, **stems**, and **leaves**. Some plants have flowers. Some plants have fruits. Name five kinds of fruits.

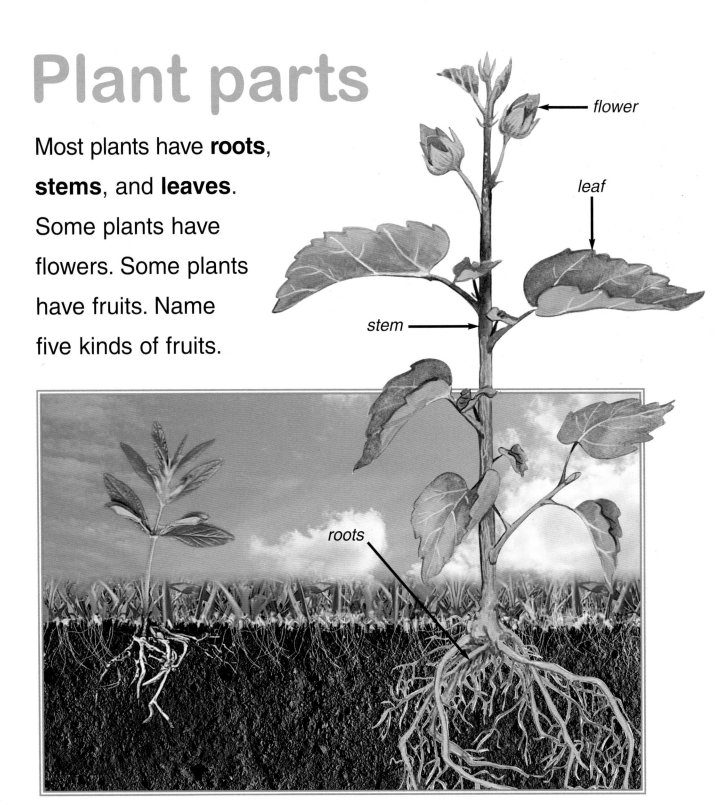

flower

leaf

stem

roots

seeds

These sunflowers have roots, stems, leaves, and flowers. They have seeds, too. Where are their seeds? This small pepper plant has roots, a stem, leaves, and fruits. Its fruits are peppers!

pepper plant

11

Plants grow

Plants grow and change. These tomato plants are small now, but they are growing quickly. Soon there will be tomatoes on the plants.

At first, the tomatoes are small and green. They keep growing.

As they grow, the tomatoes turn red. Red tomatoes are **ripe**. Ripe means fully grown. The red tomatoes are ready to eat. They are sweet and delicious!

13

Seeds to plants

Many kinds of plants make seeds.

New plants grow from the seeds.

Bean plants grow from seeds.

This plant is a bean plant.

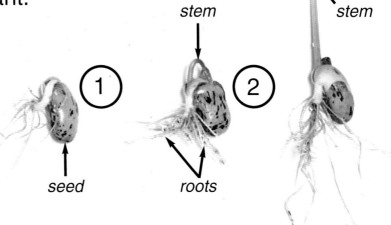

This is how a bean plant grows.

1. The seed breaks open.
2. Roots grow down into the soil.
   A stem starts to grow above
   the soil.
3. Leaves grow on the stem.
   What do you think happens next?

What is a life cycle?

The **life cycle** of a plant is how a plant changes from a seed to a grown plant. The grown plant then makes new seeds. These pictures show the life cycle of a bean plant from seed to seed.

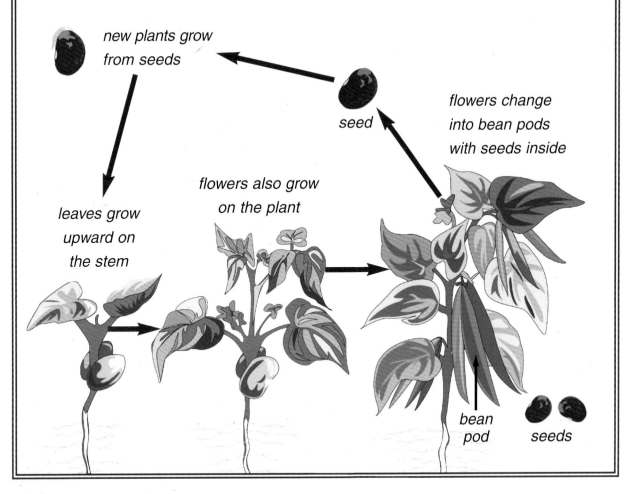

new plants grow from seeds

seed

flowers change into bean pods with seeds inside

flowers also grow on the plant

leaves grow upward on the stem

bean pod

seeds

Other ways to grow

Some plants do not grow from seeds.

They grow in different ways.

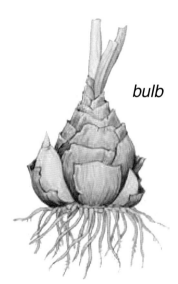

bulb

Some plants grow from
bulbs. Daffodils grow
from bulbs. The bulb
above will grow into
a daffodil like the two
flowers shown here.

16

Potatoes are fat, round stems called **tubers**. Potato plants grow from the tubers.

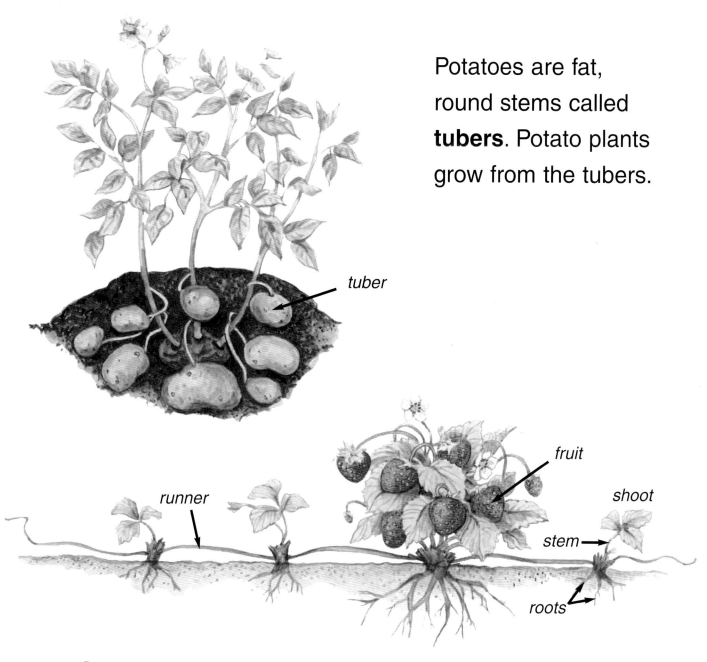

tuber

runner

fruit

shoot

stem

roots

Strawberry plants have **runners** that spread out under the ground. Small shoots grow from the runners. The shoots grow roots and stems. The shoots become new plants. Fruits grow on the new plants.

17

Plants make food

Plants are the only living things that can make their own food. Plants need sunlight, air, and water to make food. Plants take in sunlight and air through their leaves. Plants use the sunlight to turn air and water into food. Making food using sunlight is called **photosynthesis**.

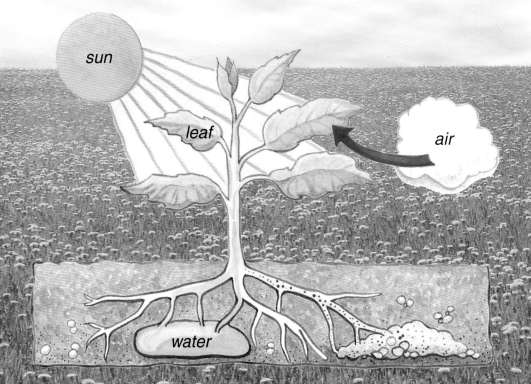

sun

leaf

air

water

Plants take in water through their roots. Their roots can be in soil or in water. Plants also take in **nutrients** from the soil or water. Nutrients help plants grow. Nutrients help us grow, too. We get our nutrients from the foods we eat.

This plant's roots take in water and nutrients from the soil.

Plants clean the air

When plants make food, they take in **carbon dioxide**. Carbon dioxide is a gas found in air. Carbon dioxide is harmful to people and animals.

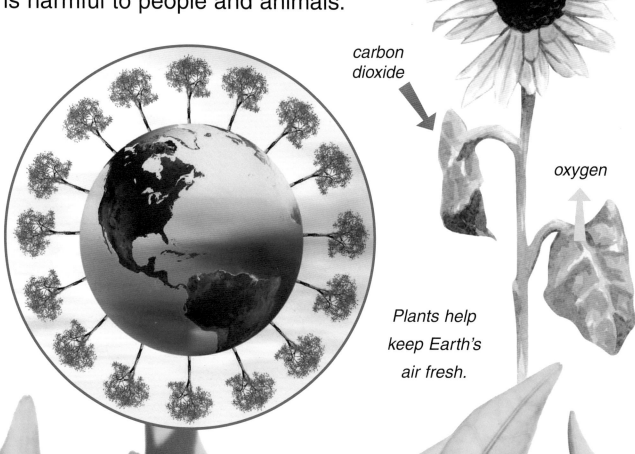

carbon dioxide

oxygen

Plants help keep Earth's air fresh.

When plants make food, they release **oxygen**. Oxygen is the gas in air that people and animals need to breathe.

Plants help clean the air by making oxygen.

We need plants!

Plants are important to all living things. Plants give us many of the things we need. Some animals make their homes from plants. This swan's nest is made from plant parts.

Trees give us shade and make the air clean. They give us wood to build our homes. We also use plants to make clothing and paper.

Most important of all, plants give animals and people food to eat. Plant a vegetable garden this spring. You will have fun watching your plants grow. You will also love the delicious foods that come from your plants!

Words to know and Index

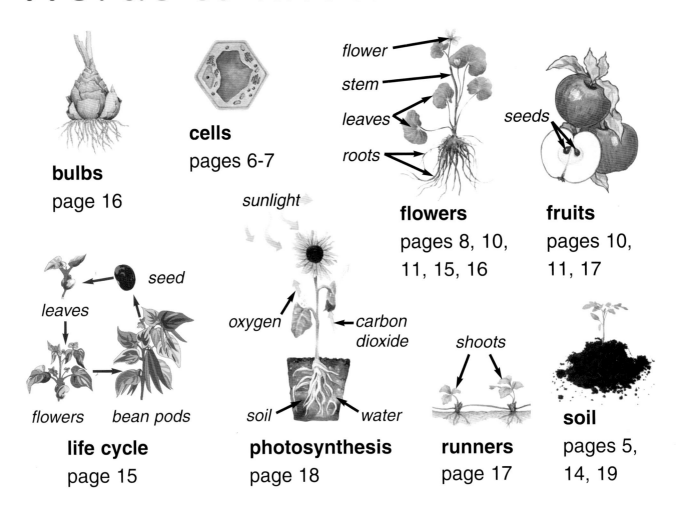

bulbs
page 16

cells
pages 6-7

flower
stem
leaves
roots

flowers
pages 8, 10, 11, 15, 16

seeds

fruits
pages 10, 11, 17

seed
leaves
flowers *bean pods*

life cycle
page 15

sunlight
oxygen *carbon dioxide*
soil *water*

photosynthesis
page 18

shoots

runners
page 17

soil
pages 5, 14, 19

tubers
page 17

water
pages 4, 5, 18, 19